GOD GIVE

ME

WISDOM

CHARLES R. JARVIS

I dedicate this book the glory of God and to all those family members, friends, acquaintances, bosses, coworkers and strangers who have shared their wisdom with me over the past seven decades.

But, most of all I wish to acknowledge the support and encouragement I've received from my wife, Brenda.

FOREWORD

Solomon wrote, "Get wisdom! Get understanding! Do not forget, nor turn away from the words of my mouth."

God Give Me Wisdom provides a wealth of wisdom derived from years of life experience, common sense, and God's Word. It is a quick read, but you will want to read it slowly and thoughtfully contemplating its many biblical admonitions and sound practical advice.

Wisdom is not valued or sought after in this information age. Knowledge is readily available, but wisdom is in short supply. In *This Little Book*, Charles R. Jarvis shares the considerable wisdom that he has derived from life's journey. All of us need to "Get wisdom." This book will help you do that. It addresses the value and content of wisdom in many different areas of life. It is not just another self-help book; it is a repository of life-learning based on eternal truth that is presented in a delightful and practical manner.

—Dr. R. Jay Waggoner
Senior Pastor, 40 years

INTRODUCTION

There's just something about longevity in life. As I approached my retirement age, after decades of working as a top-level manager and participant in community leadership, people started treating me differently. I first noticed it when young people would hold a door open for me as I entered a building. Then people would address me as, "Sir." I pondered what the heck was going on? I eventually concluded it had to be the age-old custom of respecting elders. I might have come to that conclusion as the mirror reflected my countenance while I shaved.

I had evolved, over my fifty-plus year career in the newspaper business, from frequently being the youngest person in the room, to being the oldest. It was a startling revelation. I remember, as a young upstart, hearing the "old guys" in the meetings or gatherings draw on past experiences as guidance for tackling a new project. I was young, soaking up the business, and I brashly figured I had all the answers. Frequently, however, the elders had the same knowledge I had, but they had something I didn't have. They had the benefit of having seen firsthand what we were discussing, or something very similar. They, most often, were able to merge their knowledge with their life experience and impart what I have come to realize was wisdom. My career was greatly benefitted by being able to absorb the wisdom of the "old guys."

As people would call, stop by or write a note of congratulations to acknowledge my retirement, at age 73, and after publishing a medium-size newspaper for exactly 25 years, I was touched how often they credited me with providing a measure of wisdom over the years. Me? Wise? Really? I always thought of myself as a man who had a pretty good measure of common sense and that was a great help in my decision making. Common sense and wisdom are similar, but different. We will touch on that in a later chapter. But, it seems, my common sense, at least in some people's eyes, had graduated to wisdom without me realizing it.

Every person has wisdom, but in varying amounts. And, every person is challenged with imparting that wisdom to the next generation. Wisdom is a hand-me-down. Wisdom is a legacy you leave behind. Wisdom, the Bible tells us, is more precious than gold. It is even more precious in this day and age because there seems to be a crippling shortage of it. So a prayer we all should pray is, "God, give me wisdom."

CONTENTS

CHAPTER 1

THE GREATEST GENERATION

I was born late in the last year of the first half of the 20th Century. So I grew up post World War II as an official "Baby Boomer." Actually I was born in the early stages of that generation which has been designated for those born between 1946 and 1964 — a span of 18 years.

The labeling of generations began at the beginning of the 20th Century. Those born from 1901 through 1924 have become known as the Greatest Generation. Those born in the early years of that generation became adults at the end of World War I, but those born late in the cycle endured the Great Depression and many of the men became entangled in World War II. Those who came home from "the war", the men and women who served in uniform, as well as those who served at home to supply the war, set about to work the businesses, the mills, the mines, the factories or the farms to support their families and their communities. They propagated the "Baby Boomers," children born post World War II. The Greatest Generation kicked into high gear the American economy with hard work and determination that obviously resulted from the lessons of the rigorous toil they endured through the depression years and "the war." For them, hard work was honorable work. In addition to the laborers, many of the Greatest Generation sought higher education and earned degrees in medicine, law or engineering as a prelude to making their marks in critical fields that would meet the needs of a booming economy and prosperous society.

The Baby Boomers received more education because their parents of the Greatest Generation often, especially in West Virginia where I was born and raised, had just eighth grade educations. They wanted their offspring to have an easier life than toiling in the mills, the mines and the menial jobs they had taken to provide for their families and so they could be productive citizens of their communities. The wives and husbands of the Greatest Generation, by a very high percentage, stayed together as divorce, at the time, was often viewed as scandalous. They sent the Baby Boomers to school every day, saw to it that they did their homework and, as parents, supported the teachers in their work to educate their children. With the advantage of having both parents in the home, the Baby Boomers, in large numbers, received high school diplomas and often went on to higher education.

The Baby Boomers were drilled on being self-sufficient, like their parents. They were encouraged to dream and to work hard to accomplish their hopes. Boomers Bill Gates and Steve Jobs brought us out of a mechanical society into a world of computers. Jeff Bezos and his brainchild, Amazon, changed the way the world shops. These and other Baby Boomers made the late 20th Century as exciting as Henry Ford, Harry Firestone, Alexander Graham Bell, Thomas Edison and Orville and Wilber Wright had enthused the early days of the 20th Century. Boomers Bill Clinton,

George W. Bush, Barack Obama and Donald Trump became U.S. Presidents.

The Greatest Generation's life's experiences as youth, living through hard times and surviving brutal war, gave them great opportunity to see failure on many fronts. Mistakes, wrong judgements, carelessness, and moral breakdown are authors of failure. Learning from your own failures and observing the consequences of others imparts wisdom. More wisdom is gained from others' mistakes. Nobody lives long enough, they say, to make them all himself. The Greatest Generation provided America with a wealth of wisdom, including:

- Hard work is required

- Education is important

- Faith is profitable

- Family is meaningful

- Service is influential

We owe the Greatest Generation such a debt of gratitude.

CHAPTER 2

THE VALUE OF WISDOM

Wisdom is a combination of experience, knowledge and good judgment. Real wisdom is from God above and that can come to man or woman at any age. But earthly wisdom comes from experiencing or observing the good and bad of earthly living. Earthly wisdom generally comes upon us later in life, after we have experienced many things, and some of them multiple times until we understand the good results and the bad consequences. Wisdom is fueled by understanding. Foolishness is the lack of understanding.

We all should aspire to acquire wisdom, but that acquisition is something that cannot be rushed. It will be collected gradually and eventually the way you live your life and the kind of advice you give will demonstrate your wisdom. Your family, friends and acquaintances will seek your wisdom when they see it in you.

For years as a young man I thought I had all the answers. I could accomplish anything I set out to do. I challenged myself to become good at baseball and basketball. I was at least adequate at both through high school. I wanted to be a radio announcer and accomplished that at age 13 and worked at various stations through my high school and college years. I taught myself to be a journalist by reading newspapers before seeking college training in that field, which led to a 50-year career in newspapers. In that occupation I went from often being the youngest person in the room to, for the final years of my career, being the oldest person in the room. It became evident to me that in the final decade of my work I had much more wisdom than I had back when I thought I knew everything. I really didn't seek wisdom, but I apparently acquired a good portion of it.

King Solomon in the Bible entreated his son to seek wisdom. In the Book of Proverbs, Chapter 1, King Solomon, revered as the wisest man of all time and one of its wealthiest men, wrote: "A wise man will hear, and will increase learning, and a man of understanding shall attain to wise counsels." Later in Chapter 1 he tells us, "The fear of the Lord is the beginning of knowledge; but fools despise wisdom and instruction." In Proverbs, Chapter 2, Solomon entreated his son to seek wisdom. He told him to "incline thine ear unto wisdom, and apply thine heart to understanding." He told him to search for it as if he were searching for silver or for hidden treasure. In verses 5 and 6 Solomon writes, "Then shall thou understand to fear of the Lord, and find the knowledge of God. For the Lord giveth wisdom; out of his mouth cometh knowledge an understanding."

So, if you are cruising through life tuned to your own understanding, I'm here to tell you there is a place where one can find real truth and wisdom and understanding. It's with God Almighty. It is most profitable to seek His wisdom through His word and in fellowship with Him through your prayers. He's always available. If you accept the Lord Jesus Christ as your savior he will send the Holy Spirit to indwell you and give you the understanding of God's wisdom you seek.

It is well known that you can't have wisdom without knowledge, but it is too often the case that someone has knowledge without wisdom. Knowledge is gained from schooling and study. Wisdom is acquired over time by observation. Observation gives you understanding. Understanding is the road to wisdom. Wisdom is the ability to put a lot of knowledge together with the lessons of practical experience to discern what is proper and prudent. This combination provides a picture, a clear understanding, of what the outcome would be for a particular situation. This type of wisdom is the best mortal man can do alone. Wisdom from God however has the benefit of an omniscient partner. He knows everything, including what the conclusion of any situation will be. Always ask God to give you his wisdom when considering an important direction. Paul writes in Romans a praise of God's wisdom:

"O the depth of the riches both of the wisdom and knowledge of God! how unsearchable are his judgments, and his ways past finding out."
Romans 11:33 KJV

"For of him, and through him, are all things: to whom be glory for ever. Amen."
Romans 11:36 KJV

CHAPTER 3

INFORMATION OVERLOAD

The late Charles Stanley, pastor of the First Baptist Church of Atlanta, Georgia, and founder of the widely known *In Touch Ministries,* has a wonderful sermon preserved on YouTube that says we are living in an information age. He amplifies that saying we actually are on information overload these days. Thirty years ago few could have conceived that one day we would carry in our pocket a telephone that could provide access to easily indexed information from the whole Library of Congress and a multitude of other voluminous sources. Our access to knowledge is endless, but Pastor Stanley said we are woefully lacking in wisdom.

One unknown source cleverly says "knowledge tells us that a tomato is a fruit. Wisdom tells us not to put tomato into a fruit salad."

It seems as if we are saying that gaining wisdom is a slow and arduous process. It certainly can be. Longevity of life and added exposure to the lessons of life add depth to our wisdom. But, actually, there is a simple way to begin exhibiting wisdom with one practical application which can be made at any age — *wisdom is always doing what you think is the right thing.* If you weigh the right and wrong approaches to any situation, and you chose to do what you believe to be the right thing, you can't be too far wrong. Oh, there will be occasions when you have overlooked something that will cause your choice to not have been optimal, but that lesson will lead to greater wisdom the next time you face a similar circumstance.

God is the great counselor of wisdom. God is never taken by surprise by any circumstance in our lives. He is not confounded or unsure about anything. Daniel writes in his biblical book:

"Blessed be the name of God for ever and ever: for wisdom and might are his: And he changeth the times and the seasons: he removeth kings, and setteth up kings: he giveth wisdom unto the wise, and knowledge to them that know understanding. He revealeth the deep and secret

things: he knoweth what is in the darkness, and
the light dwelleth with him."
Daniel 2:20-22 KJV

Daniel had sought God's wisdom to reveal the meaning of King Nebuchadnezzar's dream. When Daniel told the king of the meaning of his dream, he spared the lives of Daniel and his companions, Hananiah, Mishael and Azariah, as well as all of the magicians, astrologers, sorcerers and the Chaldeans, who could not interpret the king's dream.

When Daniel reported to the king what the others could not interpret, he added that God had revealed the answers to him.

"There is a God in heaven that revealeth secrets
and maketh known to the king Nebuchadnez-
zar what shall be in the latter days."
Daniel 2:28 KJV

The king not only spared Daniel, but lavished gifts and praise upon him and made him ruler over the whole province of Babylon and chief of the governors over all the wise men of Babylon.

In the first chapter of the Book of James, written by the apostle James, a half-brother of Jesus, we are told:

"If any of you lack wisdom, let him ask of God that giveth to all men liberally, and upbraideth not; and it shall be given to him."
James 1:5 KJV

How does God dispense his wisdom? Through his word, which is interpreted for you by the Holy Spirit, once you have accepted Jesus Christ as your Lord and Savior. But James cautions us in the sixth verse of Chapter 1 that we must ask in faith, with "noth-ing wavering," that God *will* impart to us his wisdom. He also, I believe, wants to use us grounded Christians to share his wisdom to our families and our acquaintances.

Wisdom is a gift from God.

"Every good gift and every perfect gift is from above, and cometh down from the Father of lights, with whom is no variableness, neither shadow of turning."
James 1:17 KJV

James continues with his theme of wisdom in Chapter 3 of his book. In verse 13 he en-courages wise men with significant knowledge to tell of their works with meekness and wis-dom. But if there is bitterness, envy and strife on one's heart, verse 14 says, this wisdom is not from above but is "earthly, sensual and devilish."

"For where envying and strife is, there is confusion and every evil work"

James 3:16 KJV

"But the wisdom that is from above is first pure, then peaceable, gentle, and easy to be intreated, full of mercy and good fruits, without partiality, and without hypocrisy."

James 3:17 KJV

CHAPTER 4

WISDOM IS TRUTH

The political realm of the 21st Century is one of total confusion. The political structure in America has changed from one of party allegiance to widely separated camps of liberals and conservatives. The perception, which as they say is reality, is that Democrats are liberals and Republicans are conservatives. That is the notion because the fringe wings of the Red and Blue parties are controlling each party's narrative. Real wisdom is required to get a glimpse of the truth as both the liberals and the conservatives have convincing arguments for and against any issue.

Knowledge is imparted to us through many filters. Samuel Langhorne Clemmens, under the pen name Mark Twain, was an American writer and humorist. He pegged it correctly when he panned dependence on knowledge with his quote: "The trouble with the world is not that people know too little; it's that they know so many things that just aren't so." If you've heard the arguments for and against climate change you have to know that some of them just are not so. Same thing with the abortion issue; should a woman have the right to end the life of a fetus in her body at any stage or does God's admonition control against killing the unborn? One or the other is just not so. I, personally, would not question God's authority on matters of his own creation.

The liberal view is that the world has changed from the Biblical days when God's commandments were recorded. This did not take God by surprise, either. Paul wrote:

"Let no man deceive himself. If any man among you seemeth to be wise in this world, let him become a fool, that he may be wise."

1 Corinthians 3:18 KJV

In this world, today's society, we find ourselves being indoctrinated by special interest groups seeking to overrule God's teachings of right and wrong. They want us to believe there is no right or wrong. They have convinced our schools to ignore moral standards and teach our children that it's all right to accept as normal, lifestyles that clearly are sinful and destructive by moral standards that have been observed for thousands of years. We are allowing this deception and we are becoming the fools that Paul writes about in 1 Corinthians 3:18. God help us, at some point, to realize this foolishness and let us become wise.

"Love not the world, neither the things that are in the world. If any man love the world, the love of the Father is not in him. For all that is in the world, the lust of the flesh, and the lust of the eyes, and the pride of life, is not of the Father, but is of the world. And the world passeth away, and the lust thereof: but he that doeth the will of God abideth for ever."

1 John 2:15-17 KJV

It is the world telling us the word of God, the Bible, is outdated. It is the world today telling us the Bible is no longer relevant. The Bible has survived centuries of attempts to discredit it and even destroy it. God knew this and warned against it.

I warn everyone who hears the words of the prophecy of this book: if anyone adds to them, God will add to him the plagues described in this book, and if anyone takes away the words of this book of this prophecy, God will take away his share in the tree of life and in the holy city, which are described in this book.

Revelation 22:18-19 ESV

Jesus Christ is the same yesterday, and today, and forever.

Hebrews 13:8 KJV

Wisdom is truth, and the word of God is true.

CHAPTER 5

ARTIFICIAL INTELLIGENCE AND WISDOM

The world, in this 21st Century since the birth of Jesus, is rapidly grasping onto Artificial Intelligence (AI). AI experiments have been ongoing since the 1950s. In the 1960s the U.S. military attempted to have computers mimic basic human reasoning, according to SAS Institute, a software generator since the 1970s. SAS says the government's

Defense Advanced Research Projects Agency (DARPA) developed personal assistant software long before anyone every heard of Siri or Alexa. The explosion of AI has resulted due to the massive amounts of knowledge that has been launched into the digitized world that can be searched and mimicked by algorithms. Computers can be programmed to seek out knowledge and experiences to obtain a reasonable outcome for almost any problem. When I began contemplating how wisdom differed from common sense, I found Sage at *poe.com*. Sage was obviously so named to represent the dictionary.com definition of the word, "a profoundly wise person; a person famed for wisdom." Sage identified itself as "a bot powered by Open AI's Chat GPT."

Also, according to dictionary.com, a "bot" is "a software program that can execute commands, reply to messages, or perform routine tasks, such as online searches either automatically or with minimal human intervention (often used in combination) ie., a social media bot retweeting certain posts; a customer service ***chatbot*** to answer product questions."

Within seconds after I asked Sage what would the difference be between wisdom and common sense, I got this response:

"*Wisdom and common sense are related concepts but they are not the same thing. Common sense is the ability to think and act in a sensible way without relying on specialized knowledge. It involves practical knowledge and understanding of the world that most people have. It's the ability to think and make decisions based on what is generally considered to be true or right. Wisdom, on the other hand, is a deeper understanding of life and the world around us. It's the ability to see things from a broader perspective and make judgments based on a wide range of experiences and knowledge. Wisdom is often considered to be a combination of knowledge, experience, and insight. It's the ability to make sound judgments about difficult or complex situations and to see the long-term consequences of one's actions. In short, common sense is the ability to make basic, everyday decisions, while wisdom is the ability to make deeper and more complex judgments."*

I was blown away by such a deft rapid response. I quickly typed another question. "Can you give me an example of the two concepts?"

Sage snapped back: *"Let's say you're a college student who has a big exam tomorrow. Common sense might tell you to pull an all-nighter to cram as much information into your brain as possible. This decision might be based on the belief that studying more is always better and that sacrificing sleep is worth it in order to perform well on the exam.*

"Wisdom, on the other hand, might lead you to a different decision. It might lead you to consider the research that shows that getting enough sleep is critical for brain function and memory retention. Wisdom might lead you to prioritize getting a good night's sleep, even if it means studying a little less. This decision might be based on the belief that long-term success in college requires a focus on overall health and well-being, not just short-term academic performance.

"So in this example, common sense might lead you to prioritize short-term academic success over long-term health and well-being, while wisdom might lead you to take a more balanced and thoughtful approach to the situation."

I asked Sage if its response was copyrighted and Sage responded that it holds no license for the material, that it was garnered from various searches of digitized documents and warned that some of the content it shares may be copyrighted by someone.

I asked if Sage could share its sources.

It replied, "*As an AI language model, I don't have access to a specific source for the answer I provided. However, the information on the importance of sleep for brain function and memory retention is supported by various studies and research in the field of neuroscience and cognitive psychology.*"

So, in a matter of seconds this bot scanned many digitized documents and composed a well-conceived response to my specific question. I guess it is highly possible that I'm not the first to ask Sage this question, "What is the difference between wisdom and common sense?" If so, this bot may have filed the answer for immediate recall. Either way, it was very impressive.

Other than using Siri on a very limited basis, this was my first foray in the world of Artificial Intelligence, and I must say, I was impressed.

A combination of knowledge, experience and insight, as Sage said, is a very succinct way of describing wisdom. Knowledge is learned, experience is gained over time and insight is the ability to combine the two into wisdom.

In asking Artificial Intelligence to explain wisdom, I sought the 21st Century explanation and what I got, virtually, was the same answer I could have gotten from the Bible.

"Who is wise, and he shall understand these things? prudent, and he shall know them? for the ways of the Lord are right, and the just shall walk in them: but the transgressors shall fall therein."

Hosea 14:9 KJV

"For the Lord giveth wisdom: out of his mouth cometh knowledge and understanding."

Proverbs 2:6 KJV

CHAPTER 6

TRAIN UP THE CHILD

Parents need much wisdom in dealing with their children and dealing with their children wisely will impart much wisdom into their children. The wisdom we show to our offspring will be lasting in their hearts and will be beneficial long after we have departed.

"Train up a child in the way he should go: and when he is old, he will not depart from it."

Proverbs 22:6 KJV

I, like most children, failed to see the wisdom of my father and mother until very late in their lives. Some of the wisdom they demonstrated to me was not realized until after they were gone. In my case, the older I got, the smarter my parents got. Had I been better at seeing their wisdom at an earlier age, I would not have made many of the mistakes that I have made. It's quite humbling when you have to say to yourself, "I guess Dad was right about that." But, that is how you take your experience, combine it with your education, from your parents or otherwise, and turn it into wisdom.

We can, and should, share our wisdom with our children and others, but there is no guarantee that they will accept it or understand it, until some situation in their life brings it back to their memory. That will give them their own "I guess Dad (or Mom) was right about that" moment.

World renown evangelist Billy Graham, according to the book *Billy Graham in Quotes,* by his son Franklin Graham, said "God gave us our children so we could prepare them to become adults." Every child is a gift from God, though not every mother or father understands that. Nor do they understand how their actions will result in significant influence on that child's life.

Wisdom should be passed from generation to generation. Some families do that with great results. Others fail miserably. The children of today are the result of parental influence that is different from generations past.

Bobby Bowden, one of the greatest college football coaches of all time, had a career that spanned more than 50 years. Bowden, as a long-time coach at Florida State University, had several players who ended up in trouble with the law. He was often criticized for giving offending players a second chance. Coach Bowden was a devout Christian man who probably was invited to speak from the pulpit of more churches during his career than any other college head coach in the history of the game. He said that he was often asked if "the boys today are different?" He would answer that by saying, "No, the boys are the same. Their parents are different." Bowden said fully 65 percent of the boys he coached over the years had no father at home.

The boys and girls of today have been given a generational moniker of Generation Alpha. It encompasses those born between 2010 and 2024. Alphas will not reach adulthood until at least 2028. It seems this generation is even more likely to experience uncertain parenting. According to an article in The Atlantic magazine by Joe Pinsker, Generation Alpha is more likely than any generation of the past one hundred years to "spend some or all of their childhood in living arrangements without both of their biological parents." Generation Alpha is likely, according to various analysts, to be better educated, be more into technology and have access to more money than their predecessors. But, from where will come their wisdom?

Many children of today are being raised by grandparents. That could be a blessing in disguise. But the social acceptability of divorce has so eroded the family structure in America that solid grandparenting is not a given for this newest generation. Some of the luckiest will have two or more sets of grandparent couples who love and nurture them. With the longer life spans of today, many children will have a greater opportunity to know their great-grandparents. Other's in Generation Alpha, however, may have no grandparents who can be in their lives with regularity and offer significant opportunities for wise influence.

Generation Alpha will be educated in public school systems that are more liberally biased than ever. The battle rages in many school systems that want to strip parents of any input or control of what curriculum will be taught. The schools seem to be pushing an agenda to encourage children to question their gender and to accept abnormal behavior that has been outside of moral standards for hundreds of years.

Alphas will have more access to knowledge than any previous generation, but will they have the wisdom to discern truth from slanted or spun advocacy? What will be the foundation of their knowledge? Those that have strong family support helping them make wise choices will have a distinct advantage toward gaining wisdom to guide them through adulthood. The Bible and prayer were removed from the school houses in the 1960s. Therefor getting Alphas grounded in faith will have to happen outside of the educational setting. But more and more parents are unwisely avoiding church and eschewing the need for God in their lives.

The fear of the Lord is the beginning of wisdom: a good understanding have all they that do his commandments: his praise endureth forever.

Psalm 111:10 KJV

CHAPTER 7

FIND WISDOM IN GOD'S WORD

The Bible is a treasure trove for those searching for wisdom. A good portion of the wisdom promoted in the Bible is found in the Book of Proverbs. Proverbs contains over 15,000 words in 915 verses. According to *biblecentral.info*, "the book of Proverbs offers a collection of texts of varied authorship that focus on the acquisition of wisdom and avoidance of folly."

Proverbs Chapter 8 presents wisdom as a woman who entreats the world to pursue her. No mortal man has explained the depths of wisdom as did God's inspired words in Proverbs Chapter 8. It's a beautiful rendition of the woman's cry to the world. I present the whole 36 verses here to adequately depict their treasure of wisdom:

Proverbs 8 KJV

1 Doth not wisdom cry? and understanding put forth her voice.

2 She standeth in the top of high places, by the way of the places of the paths.

3 She crieth at the gates, at the entry of the city, at the coming in at the doors.

4 Unto you, O men, I call; and my voice is to the sons of man.

5 O ye simple, understand wisdom: and, ye fools, be ye of an understanding heart.

6 *Hear; for I will speak of excellent things; and the opening of my lips shall be right things.*

7 *For my mouth shall speak truth; and wickedness is an abomination to my lips.*

8 *All the words of my mouth are in righteousness; there is nothing froward or perverse in them.*

9 *They are all plain to him that understandeth, and right to them that find knowledge.*

10 *Receive my instruction, and not silver; and knowledge rather than choice gold.*

11 *For wisdom is better than rubies; and all the things that may be desired are not to be compared to it.*

12 *I wisdom dwell with prudence, and find out knowledge of witty inventions.*

13 *The fear of the LORD is to hate evil: pride, and arrogancy, and the evil way, and the froward mouth, do I hate.*

14 Counsel is mine, and sound wisdom: I am understanding; I have strength.

15 By me kings reign, and princes decree justice.

16 By me princes rule, and nobles, even all the judges of the earth.

17 I love them that love me; and those that seek me early shall find me.

18 Riches and honor are with me; yea, durable riches and righteousness.

19 My fruit is better than gold, yea, than fine gold; and my revenue than choice silver.

20 I lead in the way of righteousness, in the midst of the paths of judgment.

21 That I may cause those that love me to inherit substance; and I will fill their treasures.

22 The LORD possessed me in the beginning of his way, before his works of old.

23 I was set up from everlasting, from the beginning, or ever the earth was.

24 When there was no depths, I was brought forth, when there were no fountains abounding with water.

25 Before the mountains were settled, before the hills was I brought forth.

26 While as yet he had not made the earth, nor the fields, nor the highest part of the dust of the world.

27 When he prepared the heavens, I was there: when he set a compass upon the face of the depth:

28 When he established the clouds above: when he strengthened the fountains of the deep.

29 When he gave to the sea his decree, that the waters should not pass his commandment: when he appointed the foundations of the earth:

30 Then I was by him, as one brought up with him: and I was daily his delight, rejoicing always before him;

31 Rejoicing in the habitable part of his earth; and my delights were with the sons of men.

32 Now therefore hearken unto me, O ye children: for blessed are they that keep my ways.

33 Hear instruction, and be wise, and refuse it not.

34 Blessed is the man that heareth me, watching daily at my gates, waiting at the posts of my doors.

35 For whoso findeth me findeth life, and shall obtain favor of the LORD.

36 But he that sinneth against me wrongeth his own soul; all they that hate me love death.

Note in verse 7 we find a great truth: wisdom speaks truth. Lies are not wisdom. Wisdom would never speak wickedness for how could we possibly see wickedness or lies as wise?

In verse 14 wisdom declares she has understanding and therefore she is strong. Those with wisdom are made strong by its truth.

In verse 18 wisdom is blessed and honored, blessed by God and honored by man. The blessings and honor are long lasting, enduring.

In verse 19 wisdom is more valuable than worldly riches.

In verse 21 wisdom's judgements will cause substance, good things, to pass to those that love her. Wisdom will affect coming generations when it is passed down.

In verse 30 wisdom says she was possessed by the Lord from the beginning of time and is with him now. The Lord is delighted daily by her. When we are wise, we are a delight to our God.

In Verse 35 she says we who find her will find life, and will be highly favored by the Lord.

In my view one of the strongest examples of wisdom in the Bible came from the writings of Paul.

"Not that I speak in respect of want: for I have learned, in whatsoever state I am, therewith to be content."
Philippians 4:11 KJV

The wisest among us have learned to be content with their circumstances. Contentment is wisdom learned over time. It is so easy to lament the things we do not have. "Oh, if I just had more money." "Oh, if I just had better health." "Oh, if I could just get that new car." "Oh, if I had a bigger house." "Oh, if I could just win the Lottery"

The wisdom of contentment is reinforced by Paul as he wrote to Timothy:

"But godliness with contentment is great gain. For we brought nothing into this world, and it is certain we can carry nothing out. And having food and raiment let us be therewith content."

1 Timothy 6:6-8 KJV

Jesus called his disciples to leave all of their possessions behind and to follow him. Jesus would provide, he would be enough and they would learn to be content with their circumstance. When he sent his disciples out he told them to take nothing with them:

"And he sent them to preach the kingdom of God, and to heal the sick. And he said said unto them, Take nothing for your journey, neither staves, nor scrip, neither bread, neither money; neither have two coats apiece."

Luke 9:2-3 KJV

Based on their time with Jesus, do you think the disciples went out grumbling or did they go out content with their circumstances? Jesus wanted their strength to be used in presenting the gospel, not packing worldly goods along the roads.

Some of the happiest people I have encountered in my relatively long life span have been people with very little money or possessions. But, their joy and their obvious contentment with their circumstances were surely strong influences on those they were around, including me.

CHAPTER 8

FINANCIAL WISDOM

Oh, to have had greater wisdom concerning money and finances at a much earlier age. There's a statement, I'm sure, to which many of us can relate. I started working at age 13 and over my 60 years of work I've never had a problem making money, I just had a problem of not being able to keep it. I have always admired those who are appropriately frugal; those who have been faithful in saving a portion of their income; those who have been content in living within their means; those who have made wise investments and those who have shared their treasure with their church, worthwhile missions and charities.

It would be a painful process if I were to start a list of the myriad of ways I have frittered away tons of money in my lifetime. The money spent for entertainment, vacations, helping others, mentally beneficial hobbies, comfortable homes and reliable vehicles, might seem seem like frivolous spending to the most frugal observer, but I do not begrudge those expenditures. It's the dollars spent on utter foolishness, often born from bad moral judgment, or just plain stupidity are the most regretted.

Paul tells us in his letters to Timothy that money often is a problem:

For the love of money is the root of all evil: which while some coveted after, they have erred from the faith, and pierced themselves through with many sorrows.

1 Timothy 6:10 KJV

Many mistakenly believe the Bible is telling us that money is the root of all evil, when what Paul actually is saying is that the love of money is the root of all evil. The love of money often leads to immorality and wicked foolishness. Theft, bribery, adultery, prostitution and even murder are the result of the love of money. All of those are warned against in God's Ten Commandments.

He becometh poor that dealeth with a slack hand: but the hand of the diligent maketh rich.

Proverbs 10:4 KJV

While the love of money can be ruinous, having money can be a huge blessing. It should be desired, but not coveted. It helps us obtain the necessities of life and gives us the opportunity to use it for the good of ourselves and others.

The world has set a trap for all of us, when it comes to money and finances: credit cards. These plastic wonders, in this day and age, are a curse. It is very difficult to live without them, and for many its ruinous to live with them. They are enablers for us to live beyond our means. They charge interest rates that are generally unsustainable for the card holder. In the "old days" anyone charging 20 or 30 percent annual interest could have been charged with usury, defined as an illegally high interest rate. The Mafia routinely would charge a high percentage rate per day, when someone owed money they couldn't pay back. A high credit card interest rate, routinely over 20 percent, can result in years of pay back if the card holder only pays the minimum monthly payment.

I was trapped for years in credit card debt. I finally decided to break the cycle and went to my bank and borrowed enough money to pay off the credit cards. The bank's interest rate was a fraction of the credit card's demand. I was able to wipe out my debt much faster. When that was accomplished, I obtained, from my bank, a significant line of credit that I would use when large purchases were necessary. I could repay the bank at any time and I knew it would be at an agreeable interest rate.

While there are still people who resist plastic in any form, the invention of the debit card was a beginning for me to break the choke hold of credit cards. Debit cards have been around for about 60 years, but they did not become widely used until the 1990s. Before debit cards I was buying a necessity of life, gasoline, on credit cards because I often didn't have available cash and gas stations had become leery of personal checks if they didn't know you personally. Gasoline bills piled up and at the end of the month I would only pay a portion of the bill and the high interest started running up the bill each month. When I paid with the debit card, where the money is immediately deducted from your checking account, I didn't give myself the opportunity to delay payment.

Credit and debit cards are virtually a necessity as we are in a nearly cashless society. For example, if you go to a major league ballpark today, they won't accept cash for anything, including the $16.00 (or higher) beer. Imagine if the cardholder can't pay off the credit card balance each month he (or she) will be paying

20 to 30 percent interest on that $16.00 beer. Not much wisdom in that.

The state legislature in Ohio had to step in and require high schools to accept cash for entrance to sports events. Grandparents without credit or debit cards, but who had cash, were being turned away from games where their grandchildren were playing.

We are being offered credit cards from every direction. It is possible to have a credit card for every major retailer we shop at. It one time I had a Sears card and a JC Penney card, a Mastercard and a Visa. I would get a paper bill in the mail and have a few days to pay it. I once got a bill from JC Penney for a small amount, about $6.00, as I recall. I forgot to get the check in the mail and my next bill had a $35 late payment charge. I tried unsuccessfully to get the charge removed. I apparently had been successful with that request on another occasion, so they refused. I saw the light! I immediately cancelled my account and proceeded to do the same with the other cards. I opened an American Express account with a determination to pay the full bill each month on time.

The wise use of credit cards requires that you pay the entire bill each month to avoid any interest charges and to prevent the total owed from getting out of control.

In the house of the righteous is much treasure:
but in the revenues of the wicked is trouble.

Proverbs 15:6 KJV

CHAPTER 9

BE A WISE BORROWER

With average homes costing hundreds of thousands of dollars and the cheapest of vehicles costing tens of thousands of dollars, it is difficult to live in our society without debt. Without mortgage lenders most Americans would not be able to live the lifestyle they desire. It's rare for anyone with a relatively new vehicle to drive to not have a monthly car payment. Many have to pay for their vehicle over a longer period of time just to get a payment that they can afford each month. The average car payment for a new vehicle in 2023, according to data from Experian, was $725. New lease payments average $586. Used car payments averaged $516 per month. The car payment, gasoline, maintenance, insurance, licenses and taxes makes the monthly cost of transportation onerous on many families. Taking seven years to pay off a new car that gets used an average rate of 12,000 miles a year puts about 84,000 miles on the vehicle before it is paid off. The 30-year mortgage at 5 percent interest would turn a $100,000 investment in a home into $250,000 in payments over the course of the loan. The payment would be $715 per month. Add to that taxes, insurance, utilities, repairs and maintenance, and a very modest home would cost over $1,000 per month. That's $3 3.00 per day.

I point out all of this just to emphasize the importance of budgeting and to caution you about overextending your income with borrowing. In the "old days" prudent families would use the envelope system to budget their monthly income to cover expenses. This would be difficult today because of our near-cashless society. But here's how it would work. If Dad was an only breadwinner, he would bring home his cashed paycheck in small bills. Mom would have a envelopes marked with certain expenditures. First she would put enough money away to cover the monthly mortgage or rent. If that, for instance was $100, and Dad got paid each week, she would put away $25 each week so she would have enough money to pay at the first of the month. She would estimate the money needed for the phone bill, light bill, heat bill and other utilities and have a separate envelope for each one. She would set a limit that they would spend on groceries, clothing, entertainment and place those amounts in specific envelopes. Then she would have an emergency envelope where she would designate so much money each month for unforeseen needs, such as doctor's visits, medicines, repairs, occasional purchases such as new tires, school clothes, etc. The most prudent families would also designate a percentage of the pay for savings. There might be a fund for a vacation each year and money would be budgeted for that. When it came time to pay a bill or make a certain expenditure Mom would get the money from the designated envelope. If the light bill was more than expected, she might have to borrow from another envelope that had a surplus.

There are lots of apps available these days to help with your budgeting, and budgeting is a very wise thing to do. It really is a financial roadmap to help you keep up with monthly expenses and plan for future expenditures that you will need to save for.

Another simple help is to create a spreadsheet to keep trace of all of your spending in certain areas of your regular life: Utilities, Groceries, Eating Out, Hobbies/Entertainment, Insurance, Mortgage, Phones, Cable/TV, Internet, Gasoline, Maintenance/Repairs, Clothing, Miscellaneous, Etc. Log these expenditures daily or weekly and total them each month. This will keep you abreast of how much your monthly expenditures are and where you might be spending too much, if you have to cut back somewhere.

I have never been great at budgeting. As I said in the last chapter, I never had trouble making money, I just had trouble keeping it. Real budgeting would have been very beneficial to me. But, I did do a couple of wise things which I certainly recommend. When the company I worked for offered a 401k program back in 1990, I participated by committing 3 percent of my salary to that program. It was automatically deducted from my paycheck each pay period. I never missed it. For more than 30 years I stayed with the program and amassed more savings than I ever could have imagined. The company offered, as many companies do, a contribution to my plan in addition to my salary. That was like free money. The money was invested by the financial firm that managed the 401k plan, with my direction on how the money should be invested. Over the long haul, there were more good years than bad, so my investment grew nicely. I highly recommend a savings program that is automatically deducted from your paycheck.

That way you are not tempted to skip contributing on some paydays.

Too often, I hear young people say they can't afford to put any money away. Look at these assumptions. If you are making $25,000 per year and you contribute 3 percent of your wages, about $15 per week or $750 per year in a 401k or IRA that returns an average of just 5 percent a year you would have $101,431 at age 65. You very likely will do much better than that, even with just cost of living raises. You really cannot afford not to do that. With the money coming out of your check before you get it, you really will not miss it. Your money will be working for you while you sleep!

I also devised, for myself, a quasi budget that included putting money in savings when available. Let's say I have become comfortable with only using $1,000 of my every two weeks paycheck. So when my payroll was deposited into my checking account I would leave $1,000 in my checking account and transfer the remainder of my paycheck, plus anything left over from the previous $1,000, to a savings account. I used that surplus, if needed for unexpected expenses. Then, when I would get a raise, I would continue only to start the new pay period with $1,000 and thus I saved all of the increase in pay I received. That, in addition to the 3 percent I was contributing to my 401k each pay period, made up my savings plan and the $1,000 was used for living expenses. When I paid off a car payment or any other install-ment plan, that money would then go to the savings account. It was unconventional, but actually worked quite well. However, if you are disciplined enough, I'd recommend you find yourself a good free budgeting app and use it.

***

True economy consists in always making income exceed the out-go. Wear the old clothes a little longer if necessary; dispense with the new pair of gloves; mend the old dress: live on a plainer food if need be; so that, under all circumstances, unless some unforeseen accident occurs, there will be a margin in favor of the income.

P.T. Barnum

CHAPTER 10

WISDOM OF CONROLLING YOUR THOUGHTS

I passed a sign for a mental health clinic that read "What Controls Your Mind, Controls Your Life."

That was my thought of the day for that day and for several days since. Every action and reaction of our body originates in our mind. It takes in information from our six primary senses: sight, smell, sound, taste, touch and balance. The immediate processing of that information moves our body parts to action.

The information overload in the world today, mentioned in Chapter 3, fills our minds with innumerable thoughts each day. The brain sorts those thoughts into two files: Those that we believe to be true and useful to us and those that we wish to discount or ignore. God wishes that we fill our minds with good things that would be profitable to our lives; thoughts that would abide by his commandments and lead to a worshipful relationship with the Almighty. Satan, however, wants to fill our thoughts with foolishness that would lead to selfish, immoral behavior that would result in his desired destruction of our lives and our condemnation in the life hereafter.

Do not conform to the pattern of this world, but be transformed by the renewing of your mind. Then you will be able to test and approve what God's will is — his good, pleasing and perfect will.

Romans 12:2 NIV

So, as the adage in this chapter's first sentence says, "What controls your mind, controls your life," I ask: What is controlling your mind?

Moms and Dads fill their minds with concern for their family, providing a home, transportation, health care, education, entertainment and safety. The world each day warns against being comfortable with any of those responsibilities. The cost associated with any of those wants or needs is climbing every day. Job stability is precarious at best. The world tells you to worry. God tells us to trust Him.

But what is controlling the minds of most people? The evening news? The fears expressed by their friends and acquaintances? Are you thinking about the latest mass shooting or the recent social unrest in the cities?

Even the weather forecasters are eager to scare us by pointing out the next possible storm churning in a far away hemisphere. We mortals are always dealing with the last, present or future "storm" in our lives. If our worry is bigger than our faith, life is a constant battle.

If your are like me, you have many thoughts stored in your brain that you wish you could forget about, erase or blot out from our mental files. Something in the world, detected by one of our senses, brings that bad memory back to our mental screen for primetime viewing. We have to mentally shove that memory back in its place and slam the door shut once more. Oh, for a mental delete key. Why is it that we often can't remember the details of the good experiences but the bad ones flow back with ease? Satan wants us to remember those bad things. He's trying desperately to convince us that we are not good enough to be given the grace of God. He is trying to control our lives by controlling our minds.

That is exactly why we need to fill our thoughts with good things, to leave as little room as possible for the devil to slip his mischievous thoughts into our brains.

Finally brethren, whatsoever things are true, whatsoever things are honest, whatsoever things are just, whatsoever things are pure, whatsoever things are of good report; if there be any virtue and if there be any praise think on these things.
Philippians 4:8 KJV

How can we fill our thoughts with good things, you ask?

Worry, bitterness, jealousy, coveting and fear are killers of good thoughts.

Just as we do with our furnaces and air conditioners or the oil or gasoline in our cars, we need to change or clean our filters periodically. We need to filter out a lot of the information the world is feedings us. We need to put in really strong filters to protect us from the filth, morally deprived trash that his coming out of Hollywood. The producers of movies and music seem to be stretching for the most shocking content that has never before been presented. There is little they are NOT willing to do to shock our senses and break down the moral code of America. These industries seem to encourage unspeakable violence. They promote the public conversational use of profane and vulgar words that once were totally unacceptable in our culture. They corrupt our children with violent video games and vulgar music.

For many years, I would select one movie a year to see. I admired the work of a few actors, and I do mean a few. I had to remove many very talented actors or actresses from my "must-see" list because of their public pronouncements of support or condemnation of certain social or political issues. So I would lend a light ear to the new movies that were out and select one movie a year to see. But the offerings from Hollywood these days have forced me to cut back on my once-a-year support.

The news these days seems less about useful information than it is about salaciousness. It is less journalism and more about woke advocacy. It's promotion of the growth of social issues that are antithetical to God's word is con-

stant fare. So much of a newscast is not pro-
motional of good thoughts. We should limit
our consumption of impure thoughts.

Once we have filtered out the bad stuff,
we need to replace it with good stuff. Seven-
teenth century philosopher Blaise Pascal told
the world that "Nature abhors a vacuum."
What we filter out will create a vacuum in our
minds that will begin sucking in other information. Let's fill it with stuff that passes the
Philippians 4:8 test (see above).

At about the time of the beginning of the
new millennium, God started leading me toward singing in church. I hadn't done any
public singing since my high school years
when I was in the school choir and a quartet
of friends and I had a garage band that made
a few school appearances. So I started singing
again during church services. I was led to write
some lyrics for southern gospel music. I wrote

a couple dozen songs in a couple of years. One was recorded by a good southern gospel family group and my wife and I have recorded a dozen of them.

Christian music is a great way to occupy your thoughts. When you are listening, it pushes out the unwanted noise with which the world is trying to consume us. It praises our God and savior. It teaches biblical truth. Every old hymn or southern gospel song has a beneficial message. They are like a three-minute sermon. The praise and worship music which focuses our thoughts on the power of God and Jesus floods our minds with good thoughts. Isn't it interesting that no other religions have such a wealth of music solely dedicated to its leaders? I use Christian music to keep my thoughts on a positive track.

Morning devotions are a great way to start a day. *The Upper Room* and *The Daily Bread* are great devotional guides. You can subscribe, find them on line or many churches provide them free. Some like to read a Bible chapter a day. Reading God's word is always profitable.

Prayer is a powerful tool. Prayer, simply put, is just talking to God. He wants to have fellowship with you. You can pray anywhere, anytime and he's there waiting to hear you. He will answer your prayers in his time and way, but he wants to hear from you. If it's important to you, it's important to him. Pray about it.

Heaven is full of answers to prayer for which no one ever bothered to ask!

Billy Graham

CHAPTER 11

WISDOM OF CHANGE

M any people find themselves stuck in a pattern of life that is spiraling out of control. Same stuff different day. They find themselves on that roller coaster ride of life. Their existence is a series of ups and downs and then they find themselves right back where they started from. In the "old" days people would say they were always living paycheck to paycheck. Today that would be living direct deposit to direct deposit. Some banks allow their depositors to get their direct deposit up to two days early to help pick up the slack when their money runs out before the month ends. Same story, if not worse, every month. It's a viscous cycle.

The down side of one's pattern of life is not always rooted in financial problems. That's just one of the most prevalent problematic issues of every day life. Others could be plagued by alcohol or substance abuse that knocks them down after they had just picked themselves up. Maybe their relationship with a spouse or friend goes from great to bad, then to good and soon it is back to bad again. Maybe these patterns have been going on for years, even decades.

Albert Einstein said the definition of insanity is doing the same thing over and over and expecting a different result. That is an often-repeated and old cliche, but it is just as true today as it was the day he coined the phrase. It is pretty clear that the repetition of bad habits will not change anything for the better. I had a friend once tell me that his horse had some bad habits and he was good at them. We, like that horse, get comfortable with our bad, destructive habits.

There probably have been times when these folks so affected have said, "Stop the world! I want to get off," but they don't see an open door or window through which to escape. It is possible they have been at this point many times but they saw too many problems to correct. That small voice in their ear told them it was futile to even try, they were trapped and there was no way out.

We Christians are quick to try to tell these stricken friends that the only answer is to turn their troubles over to God. Let Jesus carry the burden. We point to this scripture:

Come to me, all who labor and are heavy laden, and I will give you rest. Take my yoke upon you and learn from me, for I am gentle and lowly in heart, and you will find rest for your souls.
Matthew 11:28-29 ESV

Unbelievers, and sometimes even believers, will not have the understanding that God is big enough to really do what the scripture says. It just can't be that simple, they say. They need to see a plan of action that just might break their cycle of misery.

They need to see the wisdom in change. To stop the cyclical madness, some things have to change. There is a three-step plan that, when adopted in its entirety, will transform the most emotionally afflicted life. I have tried to find the source of this exact strategy, but I've been unsuccessful. My apologies are extended to whoever is responsible for this original thought.

The theory is that if we make these three achievable changes, our circumstances will improve.

No. 1: Change what you are doing.

As the brilliant Einstein said, we can not keep doing what we are doing over and over and get a different result. If it's drinking excessively, we have to recognize that and stop. If it's drugs, same thing. If it's arguing and fighting in a relationship, you have to stop that. If it's outbursts of anger or violence, you have to quit that. If your finances are a mess and you are not operating with a budget, make a budget for yourself (see Chapter 8). If you can't do these things on your own, you have to seek help. Accept your problem and get help. Find a good counselor, preferably a Christian counselor.

If you really want to change what you are doing, you will also need to move on to Steps 2 and 3.

No. 2: Change where you are doing it.

If the problem is drinking, you will have to stop going to the bar, even if it's your favorite hangout. You have to stop going to places that serve alcohol. If it's drugs, you can't go to the place where you get them or or anywhere they are made available to you. If you are hanging out in places where drug use is common, stay out of there. If you are spending too much money on clothes, stay away from the stores, don't rush to every sale. Stop shopping on line, it's too easy and convenient. If you are spending too much money on eating out, eat more meals at home, pack a lunch and stay out of the restaurant. Realize that a quick lunch at a fast food restaurant every day can cost you hundreds of dollars a month. Do not drive through the Drive Thru. Do you have a problem with gambling? If so, you know where you are doing that. Stay away from there. Do you have an expensive hobby that you can't really afford. Lay off of it until you financial picture can support it occasionally. Where are you spending your Sunday mornings? In bed? At the golf course? Fishing? Why not change that to an hour or two at church? It would be much more profitable and cheaper.

The next step may be the hardest of the three, but it might be the single most effective conduit to changing your life.

No. 3: Change who you are doing it with.

When I was a boy, in the 1960s at age 10 or so, I started hanging out with some boys in our neighborhood who were a little older. I followed along with them wherever they went. We would gather on a corner in the little town I grew up in. Sometimes we would loaf together into the evening hours. One evening my mother came home from working at the sweater factory where she was a sewer of garments that eventually would be sold at Sears & Roebuck stores across the country. Her boss, a Boy Scout leader in the community, had told her that he had seen me hanging out on the street corner with some boys that he said were the wrong kind of boys that I should be hanging around with. He told her if I continued to hang with those boys I would end up in trouble. I don't recall what was talked about on that street corner or even if that group did mischievous things when I was with them. I do remember, however, that some of those boys ended up in trouble. Needless to say, I was never seen in that group again and it wasn't long until I was wearing a scout uniform. It was great wisdom that my mother's boss imparted.

The people we hang with will either build us up or tear us down. If you want to stop drinking, you have to stop hanging around with drinkers. If you want to stop doing drugs, you have to stop hanging around with "drugees." If your friends are struggling with the same things you are, maybe there is a reason for that. If you are commiserating with someone in similar unfavorable circumstances, maybe you are just reinforcing your desperation. Spend less time with that person and see if that doesn't help you to see things more positively, more clearly.

When I rededicated my life to God in the mid-1980s, I had to walk away from a vocation that was done in a mostly Godless environment. I had to leave behind some really good friends who were unchurched and I was following them into places and circumstances that were damaging my testimony. Some of these friends I could trust with my very life and often times with large sums of money. Other than that virtue of trust, however, there were few other worthy social values associated with them.

So "cold turkey" I stopped doing what I was doing. I stopped going were I was going. *And* I stopped doing what I was doing and going where I was going with the people I had been associating with.

I had broken my failing pattern of life. I returned to regular church attendance. I began to associate with successful Christian people. I returned to my trained profession, worked to repair my financial situation and for the next three decades my life, though not perfect, improved in dramatic proportions.

Today I feel I am a very blessed person. Given my current situation, I can look back on my past and say I wouldn't change a thing. The mistakes and bad judgments made earlier in life have given me wisdom I would not have accepted if I hadn't had the first-hand experience of my faults and failures.

If your life needs improvement in any area, I offer the above remedy.

***

Good judgment comes from experience, and a lot of that comes from bad judgment.

Will Rogers

CHAPTER 12

WISDOM IN SPORTS

I have been a sports fan since I saw my first ball, I think it was a baseball. I love football, especially college football. I played football in the eighth grade, but really didn't love the pain that was involved so after going through the two-a-days as a freshman, I gave up playing that game. I was introduced to basketball as a seventh grader and thought my life had changed when they gave me my first pair of Converse shoes. I lettered in high school basketball. I scored 22 points in a game as a freshman, it was the only game my father ever saw me play. I truly love March Madness! I played youth league baseball, Babe Ruth League baseball and high school baseball. I pitched and played infield positions at that level. I love major league baseball and watch too much of it on television. Since I got my first transistor radio when I was a young boy, I have loved listening to radio broadcasts of baseball.

I began reading the sports pages at about age 10 when I had my first paper route. As a teen-ager, I did radio play-by-play broadcasts for high school sports. I was sports editor at my college newspaper and my first job out of college was as a sports editor of a daily newspaper. I covered sports for United Press International in two stints, including one year of covering the pinnacle of college basketball at the time, Tobacco Road basketball, in North Carolina.

I learned a lot playing and covering the games. If I have any wisdom, some of it came from my exposure to sports and its participants.

In the following, I share what I believe to be some of the best quotes of wisdom from sports figures:

- You can't get much done in life if you only work on days you feel good. *Jerry West*

- I learned a long time ago that you don't have to go around using bad language and trying to hurt people to show how macho you are. That stuff won't get you anywhere, it just shows lack of vocabulary and character. *Bobby Bowden*

91

- Winners never quit and quitters never win. *Vince Lombardi (This was my class motto at Spencer (W.Va.) High School in 1967.)*

- I've missed more than 9,000 shots in my career. I've lost almost 300 games. Twenty-six times I've been trusted to take the game-winning shot and missed. I've failed over and over and over again in my life. And that is why I succeed. *Michael Jordan*

- Remember. Every day, some ordinary person does something extraordinary. Today, it's your turn. *Lou Holtz*

- Don't complain about not getting a chance and then be unprepared when you finally do. *Joe Montana*

- The only one who can tell you 'you can't win' is you and you don't have to listen. *Jessica Ennis-Hill*

- I hated every minute of training, but I said, don't quit, suffer now and live the rest of your life as a champion. *Muhammad Ali*

- When you win, say nothing. When you lose, say less. *Paul Brown*

- If you can't outplay them, outwork them. *Ben Hogan*

- The only way to prove that you're a good sport is to lose. *Ernie Banks*

- When you make a mistake, there are only three things you should ever do about it: 1. Admit it. 2. Learn from it, and 3. Don't repeat it. *Bear Bryant*

- Success is not only for the elite. Success is there for those who want it, plan for it, and take action to achieve it. *Jim Brown*

- If you fail to prepare, you're prepared to fail. *Mark Spitz*

- Make sure your worst enemy doesn't live between your own two ears. *Laird Hamilton*

- If you see a defense team with dirt and mud on their backs, they've had a bad day. *John Madden*

- *Keep hustling, something good will happen. Joe Paterno.*

- Perfection is not attainable, but if we chase perfection we can catch excellence. *Vince Lomardi*

- You miss 100% of the shots you don't take. *Wayne Gretzky*

- Sports serve society by providing vivid examples of excellence. *George Will*

- Why hit a conservative shot. When you miss it you are in just as much trouble as when you miss a bold one. *Arnold Palmer*

- You just can't beat a person who never gives up. *Babe Ruth*

CHAPTER 13

AGE-OLD WISDOM

All wisdom resides only in one place, with God. From the beginning of time man has been in the search of it. The revelation of truth from God through man began being recorded at the earliest point of transcription. The earliest known wisdom literature dates back 2,500 years B.C. The regions of ancient Mesopotamia and Egypt produced the earliest documentation of wisdom.

King Solomon wrote the Book of Proverbs in the Bible. He is often hailed as the wisest man ever.

God gave Solomon wisdom and very great insight, and a breadth of understanding as measureless as the sand on the seashore. Solomon's wisdom was greater than the wisdom of all the people of the East, and greater than all the wisdom of Egypt. He was wiser than anyone else, including Ethan the Ezrahite—wiser than Heman, Kalkol and Darda, the sons of Mahol. And his fame spread to all the surrounding nations. He spoke three thousand proverbs and his songs numbered a thousand and five. He spoke about plant life, from the cedar of Lebanon to the hyssop that grows out of walls. He also spoke about animals and birds, reptiles and fish. From all nations people came to listen to

Solomon's wisdom, sent by all the kings of the
world, who had heard of his wisdom.
1 Kings 4:29-39 NIV

Solomon is thought to have reigned over Isreal from 970 B.C. until 931 B.C. Other practicing philosophers such as Confucius, who died in 479 B.C. at age 80, and Plato, who died in 347 B.C. also at age 80, espoused wisdom that is still quoted today. Play writer Sophocles, who died in 406 B.C. at age 92, pondered and wrote about wisdom, as did Publilius Syrus, a writer who lived the first 40 years after Christ's birth and through the crucifixion and resurrection, understood and wrote about how wisdom was gained.

Below I list several age-old quotations that exhibit or explain wisdom, as well as some much more recent ones which are old, but not ancient:

- Wise men talk because they have something to say; Fools, because they have to say something. *Plato*

- The man who asks a question is a fool for a minute, the man who does not ask is a fool for life." *Confucius*

- The greatest scholars are not usually the wisest people. *Geoffrey Chaucer*

- Only the wisest and stupidest of men never change. *Confucius*

- Three things cannot be long hidden: the sun, the moon, and the truth. *Buddha*

- It's not what happens to you, but how you react to it that matters. *Epictetus*

- Wealth consists not of having great possessions, but in having few wants. *Epictetus*

- Patience is the companion of wisdom. *Saint Augustine*

- By three methods may we learn wisdom: First by reflection, which is noblest; Second, by imitation, which is easiest; and third by experience, which is the bitterest. *Confucius*

- The greater danger for most of us lies not in setting our goals too high and falling short; but in setting our aim too low, and achieving our mark. *Michelangelo*

- From the errors of others, a wise man corrects his own. *Publilius Syrus*

- Memory is the mother of all wisdom. *Aeschylus*

- Wisdom is the supreme part of happiness. *Sophocles*

- The highest form of wisdom is kindness. *The Talmud*

- Darkness cannot drive out darkness; only light can do that. Hate cannot drive out hate; only love can do that. *Martin Luther King Jr.*

- There are a thousand hacking at the branches of evil to one who is striking at the root. *Henry David Thoreau*

- Life's tragedy is that we get old too soon and wise too late. *Benjamin Franklin*

- We cannot solve our problems with the same thinking we used when we created them. *Albert Einstein*

- A loving heart is the truest wisdom, *Charles Dickens*

- You may have to fight a battle more than once to win it. *Margaret Thatcher*

- Forget the past. *Nelson Mandela*

- Obstacles are those frightful things you see when you take your eyes off your goal. *Henry Ford*

- Don't ever make decisions based on fear. Make decisions based on hope and possibility. Make decisions based on what should happen, not what shouldn't. *Michelle Obama*

- Only put off until tomorrow what you are willing to die having left undone. *Pablo Picasso*

- Never lose sight of the fact that the most important yardstick of your success will be how you treat other people - your family, friends, and coworkers, and even strangers you meet along the way. *Barbara Bush*

- We cannot become what we need to be by remaining what we are. *Max de Pree*

- What you know today can affect what you do tomorrow. But what you know today cannot affect what you did yesterday. *Condoleezza Rice*

- The young man knows the rules, but the old man knows the exceptions. *Oliver Wendell Homes, Sr.*

- The spirit of envy can destroy; it can never build. *Margaret Thatcher*

- If you look at what you have in life, you'll always have more. If you look at what you don't have in life, you'll never have enough. *Oprah Winfrey*

CHAPTER 14

WIT AND WISDOM

The saying "laughter is the best medicine" is often attributed to American humor writer Bennett Cerf, but the concept probably springs from this scripture:

A cheerful heart is good medicine, but a crushed spirit dries up the bones. Laughter is a gift from God. Laughter is a great way to stay encouraged.
Proverbs 17:22 NIV

Actually, laughter really is great medicine. It increases the amount of oxygen-rich air you take in, your heart is stimulated and it exercises your lungs and muscles. It also increases the endorphins your brain releases, and that can mask pain. Extreme laughter also improves blood circulation and lowers cortisol levels. High cortisol levels increase anxiety, depression or irritability. Do you know anyone with those symptoms? If so, they probably don't laugh enough. The Mayo Clinic reports that a good belly laugh works out the diaphragm, the abdomen and even the shoulders, leaving the muscles more relaxed afterwards. It also gives our heart a real workout. I've found I usually feel better after a good laugh.

Below, I have assembled a few quotations that impart some wisdom and often stimulates a laugh or at least a giggle.

***

- Don't tell your problems to people: eighty percent don't care; and the other twenty percent are glad you have them. *Lou Holtz*

- *T*he optimist says: "The glass is half full." The pessimist says: "The glass is half empty." The realist says: "Either way, the glass needs refilled." *Anonymous*

- Success is the ability to go from one failure to another with no loss of enthusiasm. *Winston Churchill*

- A clear conscience is the sure sign of a bad memory. *Mark Twain*

- If you do not know where you want

to go, it doesn't matter which path you take. *Lewis Carroll*

- If you're going through hell, keep going. *Winston Churchill*

- Even if you're on the right track, you'll get run over if you just sit there. *Will Rogers*

- If short hair and good manners won football games, Army and Navy would play for the National Championship every year. *Bobby Bowden*

- Politics is the ability to foretell what is going to happen tomorrow, next week, next month and next year. And to have the ability afterwards to explain why it didn't happen. *Winston Churchill*

- Why don't they pass a Constitution-al Amendment prohibiting anybody from learning anything? If it works as good as Prohibition did, in five years we will have the smartest people on earth. *Will Rogers*

- If you find yourself in a hole, stop digging. *Bill Brock*

- You don't realize how easy this game (baseball) is until you get up in that broadcasting booth. *Micky Mantle*

- Skunks, bankers and politicians are best kept at a distance. *Anonymous*

- What, sir, would the people of the earth be without woman? They would be scarce, sir, almighty scarce. *Mark Twain*

- Find something in life that you love doing. If you make a lot of money, that's a bonus, and if you don't, you still won't hate going to work. *Jeff Foxworthy*

- No one (political) party can fool all the people all the time. That's why we have two parties. *Bob Hope*

- The road to success is dotted with many tempting parking spaces. *Will Rogers*

- Age is strictly a case of mind over matter. If you don't mind, it don't matter. *Jack Benny*

- A bank is a place that will lend you money if you can prove you don't need it. *Bob Hope*

- The future isn't what it used to be. *Yogi Berra*

- Behind every great man is a woman rolling her eyes. *Jim Carrey*

- I always wanted to be somebody, but now I realize I should have been more specific. *Lily Tomlin*

- I buy expensive suits. They just look cheap on me. *Warren Buffett*

- You are only as old as you are. *Anonymous (for obvious reasons)*

CHAPTER 15

HOMEGROWN WISDOM

Wisdom, they say, is knowing what to say and when to say it. But, some of my wisest moments have been times when when I didn't express that spontaneous thought out loud.

All of us have wisdom, things we have learned from our life's experiences. It's a fun exercise to sit down with pen and paper and jot them down. Wisdom is profitable for our own lives, but it is more profitable when shared. Real wisdom should go viral, to use a modern term. You just never know when your wisdom shared is going to really be beneficial to someone.

For instance, after many years of struggling with the lack of flexibility and dexterity, I discovered this simple exercise that has made putting my belt on each day so much easier and painless. It had never occurred to me in my 70-plus years you can put your belt on your pants before you put them on. If you are a friend or acquaintance of mine and knew this but never shared it with me, shame on you!

I am reminded each day that I am old as one of the hardest tasks I have is putting on my socks. Thank goodness it is more socially acceptable these days to go sans socks.

As a stubborn man, through considerable experience, I have learned to read the directions and I find that it really does save time and aggravation. It's the same with asking for direction when trying to drive somewhere. It took a while, but I learned to use a Global Positioning System or GPS. It took longer to accept being told what to do by that nagging female voice emphatically telling me to make a U-turn.

I've learned, and I think it is wise, to do my creative work first in the day. My tedious work later. Some days, however, I must prioritize more strenuous work earliest in the day because I have limited stamina. Once that work is done, or I've done as much as I can for one day, the rest of that day requires mostly rest. A good recliner is a useful tool.

I have found that wisdom resides in many places and the hunt for it can be exhilarating, but capturing it is the most profitable. Once it is captured, sharing it should be required.

Real wisdom is never forgotten. This thought came to me as I researched for this book. I asked google to find who might have been credited for saying it, but I got no definitive response. While it may have been said before, apparently no one documented it or claimed it; therefore I shall. Wisdom is only profitable to us if we remember it. Real, profound wisdom ought to be very difficult to erase from our memory.

I have also learned that the cost of wisdom is high when you have to pay for it with your own mistakes. It is much less expensive when you borrow from the mistakes of others. I know, however, lots of wisdom can be found at no cost in the scriptures.

If life were a game of winners and losers, the biggest winner in life should be the one who dies leaving the most wisdom behind. Wisdom buried is of no value to mankind.

It recently occurred to me that if you hire a plumber, your money goes down the drain. If you do the job yourself, your time goes down the drain. You must decide which is more valuable to you: your money or your time.

The search for wisdom to display in this little book took me to many sources. Some are identifiable. Others, not so much. The following is an eclectic series of examples of wisdom I found worthy of sharing here:

- A child that disrespects his or her parents will probably grow up to disrespect everything else in life. *J. Derek Penn, author of Diary of a Black Man on Wall Street, a book I recommend to anyone who wants to more fully understand the struggle of our country's racial prejudices.*

- What a better more efficient world

we would have if people actually did what they said they were going to do. *J. Derek Penn*

- Drinking just makes you think you are something that you are not. *Amonymous*

- Don't look back. Something might be gaining on you. *Sathel Page*

- Worrying is like paying on a debt that may never come due. *Will Rogers*

- Borrowing trouble from the future doesn't deplete the supply. *Anonymous*

- Live simply. Love generously. Care deeply. Speak kindly. Leave the rest to God. *Anonymous*

- A single conversation across the table with a wise man is better than ten years mere study of books. *Henry Wadsworth Longfellow*

ETC.

FINAL THOUGHTS

As we come to the end of This Little Book, I want to leave you, the reader, with final thoughts that provide what I believe are the two wisest things anyone can do in their lifetime.

No. 1

Accept Jesus Christ as your Lord and Savior. Do you know the precise time when you surrendered your heart to Jesus? (If you know

that you have accepted Jesus, you may skip
to No. 2) Accepting Jesus is a simple process.
First you have to acknowledge that you are a
sinner.

> *For all have sinned and fall short*
> *of the glory of God.*
> Romans 3:23 ESV

You must realize that as a sinful being we
will one day die.

> *For the wages of sin is death, but the free gift of*
> *God is eternal life in Jesus Christ our Lord.*
> Romans 6:23 ESV

You must believe that Jesus is the Son of
God and that he gave his life that you might
live.

*I also received: that Christ died for our sins
in accordance with the scriptures, that he was
buried, that he was raised on the third day in
accordance with the scriptures.*
1 Corinthians 15:3-4 ESV

If you believe on these things and pray for
Jesus to become your lord and savior, He will
accept you as a child of God, forgive you of all
of your sins and give you life everlasting. You
will have been born again and the Holy Spirit
will indwell you.

*Jesus answered, Verily, verily, I say unto thee,
Except a man be born again, he cannot see the
kingdom of God.*
John 3:8 KJV

No. 2

Point others to Jesus.

The fruit of the righteous is a tree of life; and he that winneth souls is wise.
Proverbs 11:30 KJV

Glory be to God

ABOUT THE AUTHOR

CHARLES R. JARVIS

Charles R. Jarvis began writing for a living at age seventeen when he filled in for the editor of his hometown weekly newspaper in Spencer, W.Va., as the editor was recovering from a heart attack. He went on to study journalism at West Virginia University for two years before accepting a position as sports editor of a daily newspaper. He soon was recruited to write for United Press International. His career included copy editing, writing and photography at newspapers before moving into editor and publisher positions for the last 30 years of his 56-year career. He and his wife Brenda have an active Christian ministry as lay speakers and providers of special music for church services in several states. They have residences in Farmdale, Ohio and Brunswick, Ga.

ADDENDUM

Your comments on this book are welcome and appreciated. You also are encouraged to share with us any wisdom you wish to share. Please include your name and address, email or postal mail so we might contact you if we wish to include your wisdom in a future edition of God Give Me Wisdom.

CONTACT US:

email: AndThisLittleBook@gmail.com

Postal: Golden Street Ministries, LLC

P.O. Box 2

Farmdale, OH 44417